simplify.

PARTICIPANT'S GUIDE

BILL HYBELS

WITH ASHLEY WIERSMA

PARTICIPANT'S GUIDE

simplify.

unclutter your soul

four sessions

**TYNDALE®
MOMENTUM**

*An Imprint of
Tyndale House Publishers, Inc.*

Visit Tyndale online at www.tyndale.com.

Visit Tyndale Momentum online at www.tyndalemomentum.com.

TYNDALE, *Tyndale Momentum*, and the Tyndale Momentum logo are registered trademarks of Tyndale House Publishers, Inc. Tyndale Momentum is an imprint of Tyndale House Publishers, Inc.

Simplify Participant's Guide: Unclutter Your Soul

Designed by Jacqueline L. Nuñez

ISBN 978-1-4143-9125-0 Softcover

Printed in the United States of America

20   19   18   17   16   15   14
 7   6   5   4   3   2   1

Special thanks to those who made the
Simplify Participant's Guide possible:
Eddie Adyr, Bucky Arambarry,
Jean Blount, Ashlee Eiland, Jorie Johnson, Stacey and
Bryan Kidd, Patrick Losch, Kristi and Matt Lundgren, Nancy
Mehlman, Jen Oxford, Laurie and Greg Parman,
September Vaudrey, and the
Willow Creek Community Church Facilities team

Contents

a note from bill hybels

I tend to have a pretty positive outlook, but several years ago I let the pace of my life spin out of control to the point that I found myself sitting behind the wheel of my car in a grocery store parking lot, admitting to myself the reality I could no longer deny: *I hated who I had become.*

When you stay obscenely busy for as long as I had, eventually it will catch up with you. On this particular day, it smacked me in the face. I was at the end of all my clever schemes and maneuvers: No scheduling magic was going to fix the problem I now faced. I needed more than a calendar overhaul; I needed an overhaul of my *soul*. So I cried out to heaven for help.

I wonder if you can relate. Perhaps you, too, have let the themes of *hurry*, *busy*, and *no rest* mark your life for so long that you wouldn't recognize simplicity if it showed up at your front door. It could be you've grown so accustomed to the chaos and resentment inherent in a life lived way too fast that you don't know where to begin in untangling yourself from "the way it's always been." Maybe you're not even sure you *want* to simplify; sometimes the noise and motion are comforting, if only to drown out what silence and solitude might reveal.

Only you know what your pedal-to-the-metal life is costing you these days, and only you can decide to lower your RPMs. But if you're willing to do some honest work in terms of assessing your situation—inviting God's help and taking action as His Spirit directs—then I promise you'll begin to shed the layers of madness that are keeping you from a simplified life. Take the ideas I share in these four sessions and build on them; test them out and make them your own. Then, prepare to experience life in all its fullness, as you live it with an uncluttered soul.

overview

Welcome to the *Simplify Participant's Guide*, a four-session study for small groups, designed as a companion resource to the *Simplify DVD Experience*. This participant's guide will help you *examine* the core issues that lure you into frenetic living, *eradicate* the barriers that leave you exhausted and overwhelmed, and *establish* the priorities that matter most in your life.

Each session includes seven key components that will help you leverage the principles and practices discussed on the DVD:

Suggested Reading: To help you get the most out of the *Simplify DVD Experience*, each session includes suggested reading from *Simplify: Ten Practices to Unclutter Your Soul*, by Bill Hybels, to be read in conjunction with this small-group study.

Introduction: A brief narrative that sets the tone for each session.

Conversation Starter: This ice-breaker question at the beginning of each session will initiate a group dialogue about some of the key concepts in the *Simplify DVD Experience*.

Video Notes: As you watch the video presentations, these outline notes will help you focus on the key concepts and principles discussed in each session. Use the space provided to record anything that stands out to you.

Discussion Points: These questions are designed to spark a lively discussion after the group has watched each of the video sessions.

The Challenge: At the end of each group session, The Challenge will help you begin to translate into action the principles you've learned.

On Your Own: This bonus material at the end of each session will help you incorporate into your daily life the fruit of the video content and group discussion. The three segments—*Ponder*, *Pray*, and *Practice*—may be completed all at once or spread out over the days between your group meetings.

You may discover that there is far more here than you can accomplish in a four-week group study. Take your time. Untangling yourself from the overscheduled, overwhelming web of your current life entails honest, rigorous work. It's not for the faint of heart. At the same time, simplifying your life goes hand in hand with discovering new freedom to live the life God has called you to live. This participant's guide is content-rich in order to give you a multitude of tools to help you simplify your life. But that doesn't mean you have to tackle it all at once. It doesn't even mean that you have to do the four sessions in four weeks! Your group may decide to make this an eight-week study, for example, with one week for the video and discussion and a second week to discuss what you've learned from the On Your Own exercises and The Challenge. As you prepare to begin, ask God to show you how He wants you to invest in this study at this stage in your life.

tips for groups

Whether you've participated in scores of small groups before or this is your first time, this quick, straightforward overview will position you for success.

WHO SHOULD BE IN MY GROUP?

This curriculum applies to a wide range of audiences; anyone who would benefit from a slower pace, an uncluttered soul, and a more intentional walk with Christ is a perfect candidate for your group. To determine whom to invite, consider the following three steps:

1. **Pray.** Invite God's wisdom regarding the people in your sphere of influence who stand to gain the most from a study of this nature.
2. **Think.** Consider the various types of relationships you have—including, perhaps, a spouse and children, neighbors, business associates, or friends at church. Which of these groups are a natural fit for this study?
3. **Ask.** Once you know whom you want to approach, spend a few minutes crafting a thoughtful

invitation. Why are you excited about this study? What do you hope to gain by carving out time for these four sessions? Why do you think other people will also enjoy the experience?

At its core, *Simplify* is a spiritual study that encourages participants to live in full surrender to Jesus Christ. If your group includes members of other faith systems (or no faith system), be sensitive to the extra processing time that might be required to more adequately explain tenets of the Christian faith that aren't explicitly covered in these four sessions. You can also suggest other resources by Bill such as *Just Walk Across the Room* or *Becoming a Contagious Christian*.

WHEN SHOULD WE MEET?

Most groups find it useful to meet at the same time each week for four consecutive weeks. Poll your group to learn what works. For example, if you all hold nine-to-five jobs, consider meeting over lunch once a week or in the morning before business hours. If you all have young children, you might enlist the help of a trusted babysitter in your community so that group members can focus on the video and discussion.

Be sure to allow enough time prior to your first meeting for group members to complete the reading for session 1, which includes pages 1–54 in *Simplify: Ten Practices to Unclutter Your Soul*.

WHAT DO WE NEED IN ORDER TO BEGIN?

Before your first meeting, be sure each group member has his or her own copy of the following three books:

- *Simplify: Ten Practices to Unclutter Your Soul* by Bill Hybels
- *Simplify Participant's Guide*
- a Bible

Also, your group will need to secure access to each session's videos (four total), either on DVD (*Simplify DVD Experience*, available wherever books are sold) or via online streaming (www.rightnowmedia.org).

WHO SHOULD LEAD?

Many groups find that by sharing the leadership or facilitation responsibilities, each member has a greater opportunity to become invested in the content. Consider assigning each of the four sessions prior to your first meeting, so that these leaders will have plenty of preparation time.

When it is your turn to lead, keep in mind the following three big ideas:

1. **Be prayerful.** The best preparation for leading is prayer. Thank God for the opportunity to meet and to learn. Surrender your plans to His leadership. Invite His divine intervention in each group member's life. Pray often and pray sincerely, as you set your mind and heart to the task of facilitating your group.

2. **Be ready.** There tends to be a direct correlation between the leader's thoughtful preparation and the liveliness and depth of the group's discussion. Before you show up to lead, be sure you have worked through the entire session's content yourself, including prescreening the video session that the group will watch. Sort out how many minutes you plan to spend on each element of the session (see the general guidelines below) so that the time doesn't get away from you during your meeting.

3. **Be aware.** As group leader, it is your responsibility to create a respectful environment. Here are three simple tips: (1) start and end on time; (2) keep conversations on point; and (3) ensure balanced input, both from the talkative and the pensive ones in the group.

HOW DO WE SPEND OUR GROUP TIME?

The four sessions in this curriculum have been designed for meetings that each last about **ninety minutes**. Here's a suggestion for how to divide the time, but feel free to adjust as needed for shorter or longer sessions:

Opening Prayer: 5 minutes
Conversation Starter: 5–10 minutes
Video: 20–25 minutes
Group Discussion: 50 minutes
The Challenge: 5 minutes
Closing Prayer: 5 minutes

When it's your turn to lead, be mindful of how the discussion unfolds during each portion of the meeting. If the conversation is useful to the entire group, make accommodation for it to continue by shortening other elements; if the conversation is only between two or three people and can best be had offline, take the initiative to suggest that arrangement. The goal of the group discussion is to give everyone an opportunity to express his or her views and to hear the views of others.

WHAT DO WE DO BETWEEN GROUP MEETINGS?

Participants are encouraged to take time between group meetings to complete each session's On Your Own segment, in order to personalize what they're learning. This includes The Challenge that appears after each session's Discussion Points. **Before dismissing each session, read The Challenge aloud** and make sure that everyone understands what to complete on their own before the next meeting.

If you're able, when it's your turn to lead, check in with each member prior to facilitating your session to see what questions they have, and to discover how you can be praying for them throughout the week.

KEEP IT SIMPLE

The goal of these four sessions is to lessen the chaos in your life, not add to it. As you and your group engage with this material, be sure to keep this "main thing" the main thing at every turn. If you discover ways to simplify either the logistics or the group-time dynamic, seize them! Consider this your official permission to do so.

streamline your schedule

Who Do You Want to Become?

Your schedule is causing you to become someone.
Is it causing you to become
a workaholic dad,
a chronically exhausted mom,
a distracted employee,
the "heavy one" in the room . . . ?

Or is it causing you to become
a devoted follower of Christ,
a responsible financial steward,
a formidable prayer warrior,
a faithful friend?

Your schedule is causing you to become someone.
The question is, what do you think of who you've
become?

SUGGESTED READING

Prior to meeting with your group to discuss session 1, read pages 1–54 in *Simplify: Ten Practices to Unclutter Your Soul*, which includes the following chapters:

- Chapter 1: From Exhausted to Energized: Replenishing Your Energy Reserves
- Chapter 2: From Overscheduled to Organized: Harnessing Your Calendar's Power

• • •

INTRODUCTION

It's a familiar illustration, featuring three simple materials: a handful of walnuts, still in the shell; a quantity of dry rice; and a jar.

The instructions are straightforward: Fit everything into the jar. The assumption, of course, is that everything will *fit*. As we set about our task, we pour in all the rice and then realize there's not enough room for the nuts. So we empty everything out and start over, this time placing a few nuts in the bottom and then some rice; a few more nuts and a little more rice; and then the rest of the nuts and the last of the rice. But that last quarter-cup of rice overflows the jar, and we realize we've failed again.

Third time's a charm: This time, we put all the walnuts in first. Then, as we add the rice, we gently shake the jar so that the rice fills in all the gaps and every last grain fits. Miracle of miracles, everything has its place.

And so it goes with our lives. When we get the biggest-ticket items firmly in place first, everything else finds its niche.

CONVERSATION STARTER

What is the best part of your day, and why is it so enjoyable for you?

• • •

VIDEO NOTES

Replenishing Your Energy Reserves

"Are you going to be away again tonight?"

Exhausted, overwhelmed, overscheduled

Living with a full bucket

Living with an empty bucket

Streams of replenishment

connection with God

family

recreation

satisfying work

exercise

Living in fifteen-minute increments

Harnessing Your Calendar's Power
Who do I want to become?

Chair time

Drifting vs. declaring

Crafting a God-first schedule

Additional pages for notes can be found on pages 18–21.

• • •

DISCUSSION POINTS
Replenishing Your Energy Reserves

1. The question that set Bill on a course to simplify his life came from his then-three-year-old daughter: "Daddy, are you going to be away again tonight?" Have you ever been on the receiving end of a similar

question, one that feels like an indictment of how you spend your time? How was that question phrased, and who asked it? Why do such seemingly innocent questions cut us so deeply?

2. Bill mentioned a deadly pattern he's noticed; namely, that far too many people live *exhausted*, *overwhelmed*, and *overscheduled* lives. When you find yourself suffering from these feelings, which of the following triggers is usually to blame?

Fear: You're afraid to say *no* to your boss or spouse or children, and thus you take on more than you can sanely accomplish.

Overachievement: You derive a disproportionate amount of self-worth from achieving more than you did last week/season/year, or more than what others are achieving.

Guilt: You're worried that if you do something for yourself instead of remaining constantly available to everyone else, you might be judged unfavorably.

Something else . . . ?

3. In the space provided, draw a picture of your bucket, with a line showing your current level of fullness. Discuss with the group why you drew the line where you did.

4. What price have you paid along the way as a result of living with a less-than-full bucket? Sanity, perhaps? Or inner peace? What about time with loved ones or intimacy with Christ? Discuss your thoughts with your group.

5. Bill elaborated on five streams that lead to replenishment, five ways to refill your bucket:

- connection with God
- family
- satisfying work
- recreation
- exercise

When you're depleted, which of these activities tends to refill your bucket most effectively? Which one(s) are you most craving today?

When you're at the bottom of your fullness bucket, you're dangerous. Depletion has got to stop.

Harnessing Your Calendar's Power

6. Most people shy away from the very bucket-filling activities they need most, for the simple reason that they're too busy to engage in things that don't seem mission-critical in their lives. Can you relate? Take a look at your answer to the previous question, and then describe for the group what tends to get in the

way—from a scheduling perspective—of your enjoying that category of involvement more frequently.

Here are a few examples to help you get started:

Connection with God: "I'd love to have a 'quiet time' with God every morning, but I have to be at work at eight, and by the time I get myself going and get the kids off to school, I'm already running ten minutes late."

Family: "It would be nice to be together as a family more often, but with the kids' activities and my husband's travel schedule, it's not a possibility right now."

Satisfying work: "My job is a soul-squelcher that leaves me beat by day's end. The last thing I want to think about when I finally get home is searching for another job. I keep telling myself that I should just be grateful; in this economy, at least I have a job."

Recreation: "Huh? When exactly is that supposed to happen?"

Exercise: "My roommate gets up every weekday morning and heads to the gym at 6 a.m. I applaud her dedication, but honestly, I need the extra sleep."

Christ followers think differently about time; they understand that without conscious intervention, the pattern of being chronically overscheduled ensures that the priorities they care about most will take a backseat to the urgent priorities of others every time.

7. Sometimes it's easier to help others overcome the obstacles they face than to rightly evaluate solutions for ourselves. Based on the answers given to question 6 on the previous page, discuss ideas you have for how others in the group can work through the things that tend to get in their way and keep them from living replenished lives. Offer your suggestions with gentleness and humility, and be willing to hear what others say about your obstacles.

By putting God first and keeping your priorities on track, you can live out your full potential and experience the abundant life that God promises. You can become the person He is inviting you to become, one calendar square at a time.

THE CHALLENGE

Get Going on a God-First Schedule

[Leader for this session, read this part to the group:] *The challenge this week is to get going on a God-first schedule. The first step is not to consider what you want to get done, but rather to decide who you want to become.*

So, what is it for you? Do you want to become . . .

- *a more present spouse?*
- *a more devoted parent?*
- *a more fiscally responsible individual?*
- *a more grateful employee?*
- *someone who can take the stairs two at a time without gasping for breath at the top?*
- *less of a stranger to God?*

Once you have determined what kind of person you want to become, evaluate your weekly calendar through that lens. As you accept commitments and create your to-do lists, invite God's input by asking Him to show you how your involvements will move you closer to or further away from the person you want to become. At our next meeting, be prepared to share which replenishment stream you chose and your means of pursuing it.

[Leader: At this point, you may end the group meeting with a closing prayer. The rest of the exercises in this session are for group members to complete on their own.]

Your Turn

How did you answer the question, *What kind of person do I want to become?* Record your thoughts in the space following and evaluate the coming week's schedule through that lens. Over the next few days, as you accept commitments and jot down things to do, invite God's input by asking Him to show you how each of your involvements will move you closer to the person you want to become. If it helps, it stays on the calendar; if it doesn't help, it goes.

To help you begin, look back at your answer to question 5 in the Discussion Points section: Which replenishment stream do you crave most today? Now, think of one way you can incorporate that activity into this week's schedule.

If you need a little inspiration, consider the following ideas:

Connection with God: "This week, I'm going to forgo scanning online news sites first thing in the morning and use those twenty minutes to read the Bible and pray instead."

Family: "My kids' intense sports schedules aren't going to change anytime soon, but this week, I'm going to take them out for breakfast on Saturday, before games and practices begin. It's a start, anyway."

Satisfying work: "I can't stand my job. But this week, I'm going to work on adjusting my attitude to one of gratefulness instead of playing into my misery. I'm actually going to *schedule* gratitude breaks throughout my day, times when I stop working for five minutes, roam around the office, and find someone to encourage, something to clean up, or some way I can help out a colleague."

Recreation: "My wife and I used to go rock climbing before we had kids. A new rock climbing gym just opened in our area, and this week, I'm kidnapping her—kid-free!—for a recreational date night."

Exercise: "I'm going to give up that last hour of sleep two mornings this week and head to the gym with my roommate. Here's hoping it's true that exercise gives you energy. I'm going to need it."

In the space below, identify your own replenishment stream and how you plan to pursue it this week.

My replenishment stream: _____

_____

Means of pursuing it: _____

_____

To delve more deeply into the concept of replenishment, read pages 16–28 in *Simplify: Ten Practices to Unclutter Your Soul*.

session 1

on your own

The goal of this section is to help you incorporate the video content and group discussion material into your daily life. The three segments—*Ponder*, *Pray*, and *Practice*—may be completed all at once or spread out over the days between your group meetings.

Ponder

Set aside time before your next group meeting to reflect on the following questions. You'll find additional space for journaling on pages 18–21.

> How full is your "bucket" these days? Are you satisfied with your honest answer here?

> When you hear the words *exhausted, overwhelmed, and overscheduled*, what thoughts come to mind? How well do these words describe you?

What do your recent practices reveal about your
true beliefs regarding the five streams of
replenishment—connection with God, family,
satisfying work, recreation, and exercise?

What does a God-first schedule look like to you?

_____

What refuels you? What restores your energy levels? What
inspires you? What is your bucket-filler?

_____

Pray

Think back on a time when you felt intimately connected
with God. Scripture calls this "abiding" with Him, as a vine
abides in its branch. On the lines at the end of the session, consider jotting down a prayer to God, asking Him to
recapture your attention in the same way you were capti-
vated back then, back when you felt that vine-to-branch
closeness.

Then, lean in. Ask God earnest questions about who
He is calling you to be, and what implications to your daily
and weekly schedule will necessarily flow from that divine

vision. In *Simplify*, Bill writes, "When I'm really connected with God, I'm far less concerned about other people's opinions of me or their plans and expectations for my life. I'm quicker to stay on God's agenda." Perhaps you'll find the same to be true for you.

Practice

God promises to populate the deserts of this world—both literal and figurative—with dense, lush vegetation.

> In the desert, I will plant cedars, woody acacias,
>   myrtles, and olive trees.
> I will establish great cypresses to flourish in the
>   desert places,
>   plant oaks and pine trees side by side.
>
> They'll see all this and understand. They'll ponder
>   together
>   and come to know that it is the power of the Eternal
>   One that produced this.
> They will know that the Holy One of Israel created it.
> Isaiah 41:19-20, TVB

1. If you were to describe the "empty bucket" places in your life right now—just betweesn you and God—what kinds of desperate, dusty deserts would you mention?

2. God says He is the one who causes desert places to flourish. If this is true, why do we who say we love God spend so much time and energy trying to bring about that flourishing on our own?

3. What would it look like this week to turn over the flourishing of your life to God?

session 1

NOTES

_____

_____

_____

_____

_____

_____

_____

_____

_____

_____

_____

_____

_____

_____

NOTES

_____

_____

_____

_____

_____

_____

_____

_____

_____

_____

_____

_____

_____

_____

_____

NOTES

_____

_____

_____

_____

_____

_____

_____

_____

_____

_____

_____

_____

_____

_____

_____

_____

_____

NOTES

_____

_____

_____

_____

_____

_____

_____

_____

_____

_____

_____

_____

_____

_____

_____

_____

_____

_____

spend wisely

Being Satisfied with Job and Money

Time and money, money and time:
If there are two resources we're encouraged to
*   steward well,*
these would be the two.

"Don't wear yourself out trying to get rich," Proverbs
*   23:4 says.*
That is, "Know when to quit."

And so, an invitation: Simply quit.
Quit straining.
Quit striving.
Quit positioning.
Quit vying.
Quit slaving.
Quit running.
Quit working so hard to impress.

Today is the day for simplicity.
Today, invest your life well.

SUGGESTED READING

Prior to meeting with your group to discuss session 2, read pages 55–107 in *Simplify: Ten Practices to Unclutter Your Soul*, which includes the following chapters:

- Chapter 3: From Overwhelmed to In Control: Mastering Your Finances
- Chapter 4: From Restless to Fulfilled: Refining Your Working World

• • •

INTRODUCTION

The fisherman steered his small boat toward the dock of the small, coastal Mexican town, where a successful business-man happened to be visiting. The businessman, noticing a batch of robust yellowfin tuna in the bottom of the boat, complimented the fisherman on his day's catch.

"How long were you out?" asked the businessman.

"Oh, not long," the fisherman replied.

The businessman was intrigued. "Why not stay out longer and catch more fish?"

"This is enough."

The businessman wasn't tracking. "What do you mean, this is enough? You could be making a *killing* out there! What could be better than that?"

The fisherman grinned. "What's better? Well, let's see. Every day, I get to sleep late. I fish awhile. I play with my children and take a siesta with my wife, Maria. We go for a stroll into the village in the evenings, have a glass of wine, play guitar with friends, dance, talk with people we happen to meet, laugh. . . . It's a pretty good life, if you ask me."

The businessman scoffed. "Listen, I have an MBA from Harvard and could really help you here. You should spend more time fishing, and with your proceeds, get yourself a bigger boat. With that increased operation, you could afford a whole fleet of fishing boats and eventually open your own cannery. You could then move from this tiny town to central Mexico and maybe even to the United States, where you could run an entire enterprise."

The fisherman asked, "Señor, how long will this plan take?"

"Oh, not long. Fifteen to twenty years."

"But then what?" the fisherman asked.

"That's the best part! When the time is right, you'd announce your IPO, sell your company stock to the public, and become a *very* rich man. You'd make millions!"

"Then what?" asked the fisherman.

"Then you could retire!" cheered the businessman. "You could move to the coast, live life on your own terms, have not a care in the world!"

"But señor, isn't that what I'm doing right now?"

CONVERSATION STARTER

Describe a time when you spent too much time or money on something and later regretted it. Why did it feel worth it at the time?

— • • • —

VIDEO NOTES

Mastering Your Finances

All we have comes from God's hand

Living within God's provision level

Contentment vs. debt

Priority test: getting from A to B (to C)

What kind of "idiot" do you want to be?

The 10-10-80 plan

Winter is coming

Refining Your Working World
The passion alignment

The culture alignment

The challenge alignment

The compensation alignment

Additional pages for notes can be found on pages 44–47.

• • •

DISCUSSION POINTS

Mastering Your Finances

1. Respond to the assertion "All we have comes from God's hand." What influences and personal life experiences shape your opinion here?

2. Read the following descriptions. Where would you say you've spent most of your financial life, as an "A to B" person or as an "A to B to C" person? Given the same two options, where would you say you are today?

   A▶B "I need 100 percent of my income to get from where I am to where I want to go."

   A▶B▶C "I'm going to trust God's wisdom that I can get where I need to be on 90 percent of my income. I'm going to tithe the first 10 percent to Kingdom work, believing there will be increased favor for me because of my faithfulness."

Contentment can be cultivated.

3. Based on your own life experience, what is the connection between financial peace and peace in every area of life?

Refining Your Working World

4. Which of the four workplace alignments resonates most with you? Here's a quick recap:

Passion: You love what you do so much that you jump out of bed each morning eager to do it, and you're blown away that someone actually pays you for the work you do.

Culture: This refers to the environmental tenor of an organization, the "vibe," the backdrop against which you live out your passion.

Challenge: This describes the intersection between the work you do and the skill, talent, and enthusiasm you have to accomplish it.

Compensation: The fair exchange (monetary or otherwise) for the work you do.

5. What internal obstacles (fears, doubts, insecurities, etc.) or external obstacles (lack of job opportunities, cutbacks because of a down economy, etc.) keep you from pursuing alignment in all four areas more fervently?

You're going to spend at least a third of your life at work. Why not look for a job that will meet your passion, culture, challenge, and compensation needs?

---

6. What were your thoughts as you viewed Eddie's story (in this session's video) of switching careers midcourse? Whether your work occurs in a corporation, at home, on a playing field, in a church, or somewhere else entirely, is there a radical change

in your work life you wish you had the courage to make? Discuss your thoughts with the group.

7. What effect do you think simplifying your working world might have on your ability to simplify your finances? On the flip side of the coin, how might streamlining your finances provide you with the courage you need to more effectively align your working world?

8. Complete this sentence with your group: *In either my financial world or my working world, one change I know I would benefit from immediately is . . .*

What adventure is God calling you to? Trust Him. He won't lead you astray.

THE CHALLENGE

Get Honest about Money and Work

[Leader, read this part to the group:] *The challenge this week is to get honest about our money and our work. This week, we'll be answering questions about financial reconciliation, workplace alignments, and actions we can take to simplify our finances and our work life.*

To help us begin to think along those lines, let's answer the following questions with the group:

> *On a scale of 1 to 10 (1 = despair; 10 = delight), as you survey the overall landscape of your financial circumstances, how pleased are you with what you see?*

> *On a scale of 1 to 10 (1 = despair; 10 = delight), as you survey the overall landscape of your job satisfaction, how pleased are you with what you see?*

[Leader: At this point, you may end the group meeting with a closing prayer. The rest of the exercises in this session are for group members to complete on their own.]

Your Turn

PART ONE: "YOUR" MONEY

Review the five beliefs of financial reconciliation that follow and answer the questions. Feel free to use a journal or the note pages at the end of this session if more space is needed.

Five Beliefs of Financial Reconciliation

1. *All I have comes from God.*

    How much do you really believe this?

    How do your spending patterns bear out this belief?

    Even after you've worked hard to earn a paycheck, do you truly believe those funds come from God's hand?

2. *I live joyfully within God's current provision for my life.*

    Are you striving after more money?

How would those who love you answer that question about you?

In the depths of your soul, are you content with the provisions God has made for you?

Would others who know you well describe you as "contented" financially?

3. *I honor God by giving the first tenth of all my earnings to His purposes in the world.*

    Do you?

    Do you play games with your tithe, such as applying "funny math" to your paychecks or attaching conditions to your giving ("God, I'll give You this money, if You . . .")?

    What is your honest attitude toward tithing?

What influences or experiences shape your beliefs about tithing?

4. *I set aside a portion of all my earnings for emergencies, giving opportunities, and my later years.*

    If disaster struck tomorrow, how prepared financially would you be?

    What keeps you from being more faithful to build your savings account?

    What keeps you from being more generous with the money God has entrusted to you?

How much is your financial ineffectiveness or negligence going to cost those who love you, if and when an unforeseen emergency unfolds?

5. *I live each day with an open ear toward heaven, eager to respond to any whisper from God about my resources.*

   When was the last time you heard from God about a need you could help meet? Did you follow through to meet it? Why or why not?

   What divine adventures might you be missing if you have not fully given yourself over to this way of life?

PART TWO: YOUR WORK

Review the four workplace alignments below and answer the questions.

The Four Workplace Alignments

1. *Passion*

   Do you really, really like what you do?

   What would make you enjoy your work more?

2. *Culture*

   Is the setting for your work a healthy one?

   In what ways can you contribute to the health of your workplace culture? Are you doing those things now? If not, why not?

3. *Challenge*

   In a given week, how challenged are you in your role?

How challenged can you afford to be in this season?

What needs to happen for you to operate more often at that "appropriately challenged-plus" level?

4. *Compensation*

Is the compensation you receive fitting for the work you do?

Is the compensation you receive fitting for the passion you feel for your work?

What needs to happen to bring this area into alignment? With whom do you need to meet? What words do you need to say? What prayers do you need to pray?

PART THREE: TAKE ACTION TODAY

Review your answers to the questions in the first two parts. In the space provided, jot down the action items that come to mind as you address these issues. A few examples have been provided.

Next, select a handful of the action items you've identified and make a plan for getting started *today*. Strike while the iron is hot. You won't regret pulling these two key areas of your life—finances and work—into alignment.

Things I Can Do This Week to Simplify My Finances and Working World:

Money: Enact a spending freeze on all nonessential items.

Work: Talk to someone who is doing the job I wish I had.

Money: Tithe to the church I attend. Be an A ▶ B ▶ C "idiot" this week!

Work: Seek out ways to be a culture builder instead of a culture buster.

To delve more deeply into the principles of financial rec-onciliation, read pages 80–82 in *Simplify: Ten Practices to Unclutter Your Soul*. For more on assessing your work align-ments, see page 107.

Life is short. Don't waste another minute ignoring God's tap on your shoulder.

---

on your own

This section is intended to help you incorporate the video content and group discussion material into your daily life. The three segments—*Ponder*, *Pray*, and *Practice*—may be completed all at once or spread out over the days between your group meetings.

Ponder

Set aside time before your next group meeting to reflect on the following questions. You'll find additional space for journaling on pages 44–47.

What do you wish were true of your financial situation? What aspects of your money management need the most attention?

When you hear stories such as Nancy's, from this session's video—stories of people who have mismanaged money, lost it all, and paid a steep price as a result—what thoughts rush to mind?

How do you feel—really—about your working world?

What course corrections have you been postponing that need to be seriously considered today?

Truth is your friend. You will not regret taking honest stock of the important issues in your life.

Pray

Steal away for a few minutes of uninterrupted prayer time. Ask God for His thoughts on the "ponder" questions above. What does *God* wish were true of your financial situation? Does He wish you'd be honest in your dealings? More self-controlled when spending on unnecessary things? More generous? Something else?

What does God think about your work situation? Are you at the right challenge level? Are you in an environment that adds vitality to your life, or one that drains it away?

Ask God for wisdom, and He will grant it. Listen closely as He directs your steps.

Some of you were locked in a dark cell, cruelly confined behind bars. . . . Then you called out to God in your desperate condition; he got you out in the nick of time. He led you out of your dark, dark cell, broke open the jail and led you out. (Psalm 107:10, 13-14, MSG)

Practice

If there are two circumstances that can feel eerily similar to a prison cell, they are (1) financial bondage and (2) an unsatisfying work situation. Read Psalm 107:1-22 in your Bible and answer the questions below.

1. In regard to your money or your workplace contribution, in what ways do you feel as if you're in a dark cell? What "prison bars" do you wish God would break open for you? What would freedom look like to you?

2. What words would you use to tell God of your trust in His plan, of your belief that He has good things in store for those who are faithful to His will and His ways?

3. When have you most recently experienced the sensation of knowing darkness and then knowing light? Consider holding on to that clear, crisp image as you journey toward simplicity this week. You were designed to live in the light (see Matthew 5 and 6).

session 2

NOTES

_____

_____

_____

_____

_____

_____

_____

_____

_____

_____

_____

_____

_____

_____

_____

_____

NOTES

_____

_____

_____

_____

_____

_____

_____

_____

_____

_____

_____

_____

_____

_____

_____

_____

_____

_____

NOTES

_____

_____

_____

_____

_____

_____

_____

_____

_____

_____

_____

_____

_____

_____

_____

_____

_____

NOTES

_____

_____

_____

_____

_____

_____

_____

_____

_____

_____

_____

_____

_____

_____

_____

_____

strengthen your relationships

Conversations That Simplify Life

It's important to order the externals,
to streamline schedules and stick to a budget,
to take pains to sort out workplace fit.
But it's only half the goal.
It's important to order the externals,
but there's an inner world to unclutter as well.
What's true of your inner world today,
that place where thoughts and feelings and emotions
     choose to reside?
If we could peek inside, what would we find?
Tenderness and gentleness and kindness—
or egotism, narcissism, and pride?
Authenticity, vulnerability, and openness—
or outright obsession with what other people think?
A spirit of grace, of ready forgiveness—
or bitterness and stuffed-down rage?
The externals certainly matter.
But the inner world, too, must be addressed.

SUGGESTED READING

Prior to meeting with your group to discuss session 3, read pages 109–204 in *Simplify: Ten Practices to Unclutter Your Soul*, which includes the following chapters:

- Chapter 5: From Wounded to Whole: Making Room for Forgiveness
- Chapter 6: From Anxious to Peaceful: Conquering Your Fears
- Chapter 7: From Isolated to Connected: Deepening Your Relational Circles

• • •

INTRODUCTION

The report cards of yesteryear were on to something, it seems, when they made room for a grade associated with "plays well with others." Yes, there were also slots for grades in math and science, in reading and music and penmanship. But even of those who soared in all their book work, we wanted to know, *Can you get along with other people?*

Scripture prioritizes others-mindedness as well. In scores of verses, we learn that we are to love one another, forgive one another, tell one another the truth. We're to serve one another and encourage one another and live in harmony with one another all of our days. We're to treat one another with tenderness, with kindness, with the same treatment we hope to get. We're to do these things because they bring honor to God and because they lead to a simplified life.

CONVERSATION STARTER

What characteristics do you most value in a friend?

• • •

VIDEO NOTES

Conquering Your Fears

Fear as a disrupter to peace

2 Timothy 1:7

Deepening Your Relational Circles

Pruning friendships

Taking relationships to a deeper level

The gift of biblical community

Making Room for Forgiveness
What we do when we've been wronged

Category 3 wrongs

Category 2 wrongs

Category 1 wrongs

Additional pages for notes can be found on pages 65–69.

— • • • —

DISCUSSION POINTS
Conquering Your Fears

1. We all have certain fears that others might find funny or irrational; but they are real fears, debilitating fears, fears that keep you imprisoned to Satan's lies, and they are anything but funny. What thoughts did you

have as you listened to Jen's story at the beginning of the video?

The power of fear begins to diminish only when a person takes the time to understand its origins, expose its lies, and face it head-on.

---

2. Second Timothy 1:7 says, "The Spirit God gives us does not make us timid, but gives us power, love and self-discipline" (NIV). When have you experienced this promise firsthand?

3. Which of the following promises of God do you wish you lived by more often, and why?

"I know the plans I have for you," says the Lord. "They are plans for good and not for disaster, to give you a future and a hope."
Jeremiah 29:11

[Jesus said,] "Come to me, all you who are weary and burdened, and I will give you rest."
Matthew 11:28, NIV

Those who trust in the Lord will . . . soar high on wings like eagles. They will run and not grow weary. They will walk and not faint.
Isaiah 40:31

This same God who takes care of me will supply all your needs from his glorious riches, which have been given to us in Christ Jesus.
Philippians 4:19

Nothing in all creation will ever be able to separate us from the love of God that is revealed in Christ Jesus our Lord.
Romans 8:39

All who listen to me [Wisdom/God] will live in peace, untroubled by fear of harm.
Proverbs 1:33

If you confess with your mouth that Jesus is Lord
and believe in your heart that God raised him from
the dead, you will be saved.
Romans 10:9

Is there another promise (verse) you would add to the list?

Deepening Your Relational Circles

4. In what ways can you relate to the idea of being led
   down a harmful path by people you thought were
   your friends? Have you ever been the friend who led
   another astray? Discuss your thoughts with the group.

5. As you survey your current relational world, what
   "pruning" do you believe needs to occur? What has
   kept you from working through that pruning process
   before now?

6. What has your firsthand experience looked like as it
   relates to "biblical community"—the practice of knowing

others and being known, serving others and being
served, loving others and being well loved, and so forth?
What changes to your priorities, your schedule, or
your attitude would help you lean into the wisdom and
camaraderie of the other Christ followers you know?

No wonder the psalmist says, "How wonderful, how
beautiful, when brothers and sisters get along!" (Psalm
133:1, MSG). Biblical community is one of the richest
experiences in life.

Making Room for Forgiveness

7. From this session's video, what did you make of Greg
   and Laurie's decision to forgive the driver who hit and
   killed their daughter? How do you think you would
   have responded had you been in their situation?

8. Most followers of Christ want to be forgiving people;
   people who don't carry grudges; people who,

understanding the grace they've been given, choose to lead their lives in a grace-giving vein. Talk about how it feels to be a person of grace, a person who is slow to be offended and quick to forgive. Describe a time when you have lived out this vision for the Christ-following life. What felt right about your gracious response?

You can tell a lot about people by what they do after they've been wronged.

---

9. In your Bible, read the parable in Matthew 18:21-35. As much as we want to be people of quick forgiveness, God has had reason, at one time or another, to ask all of us the same question the master asks of the servant: "Shouldn't you have had mercy on your fellow servant just as I had on you?" (Matthew 18:33, NIV). What thoughts come to mind as you consider that penetrating question?

10. Give an example of an offense you have been hanging on to that you wish you could release to the capable hands of God. What fears or obstacles would you have to overcome in order to release it today?

Peter came to Jesus and asked, "Lord, how many times shall I forgive my brother or sister who sins against me? Up to seven times?" Jesus answered, "I tell you, not seven times, but seventy-seven times." (Matthew 18:21-22, NIV)

THE CHALLENGE

Say What You Need to Say

[Leader, read this part to the group:] *The challenge this week is to say what you need to say in a key relationship. To prepare your heart for that encounter, complete the following sentence aloud before we end our group time for today:* **The one thing I look forward to gaining as a result of uncluttering my relational world is** _____

_____

_____.

[Leader: At this point, you may end the group meeting with a closing prayer. The rest of the exercises in this session are for group members to complete on their own.]

Your Turn

In all three of the secondary interviews in this session's video, the path to relational simplification was paved with conversations—hard conversations, thoughtful conversations, honest conversations, timely conversations. Jen, the woman who feared telling her future husband that she had contracted an STD in college, ultimately chose to sit down with him and talk. Patrick, the man who had been sidelined by drugs and alcohol for too many years, ultimately reached out to another person going through recovery and initiated a conversation that began with three powerful words: *I need help*. And then we met Greg and Laurie, the couple who lost their child in a car accident. What an incredible choice it was to seek out the other driver, knock on his front door, and begin the dialogue with, "I came to forgive you in the name of Christ."

Relationships get simplified when we say what needs to be said. This week, it's your turn. As you scan the horizon of your relational world, where do you see issues that might be resolved, if only you'd gather courage and choose to talk?

What needs to be said? And to whom do you need to say it? Your challenge this week is to put action behind your answers to this pair of probes.

To delve more deeply into the concept of forgiveness, read pages 109–137 in *Simplify: Ten Practices to Unclutter Your Soul*. For more on conquering your fears, see pages 139–168. For input on deepening your relational circles, see pages 169–204.

session 3

on your own

This section is intended to help you incorporate the video content and group discussion material into your daily life. The three segments—*Ponder*, *Pray*, and *Practice*—may be completed all at once or spread out over the days between your group meetings.

Ponder

Set aside time before your next group meeting to reflect on the following questions. You'll find additional space for journaling on pages 65–69.

> Would you describe your relational world these days as straightforward and simple, or as chaotic and complex? Are you satisfied with your situation? Why or why not?

Regarding three key areas where relationships get sideways—being fearful about what others will think, being surrounded by false friends, and being unwilling to forgive—where do you stand to make the biggest strides? Which of these three areas needs the most attention from you?

What will you have to let go of in order to embrace simplified relational living? Your pride? Your need to be right? Your insatiable appetite for justice? Anxiety over people knowing the "real" you? Something else?

If you want to live with a less-cluttered soul, then pursue peace, reconciliation, and resolution in your relationships.

Pray

Spend a few moments praying about the relationship(s) in your life for which you *least* feel like praying. Has someone wronged you? Disparaged your name? Frustrated your plans? Failed to meet your expectations? Whoever the person—and whatever the situation—take time now to jot down prayerful thoughts to God. Need help getting started? Consider praying the words of Psalm 1 on his or her behalf. Pray that he or she would be "like a tree planted by streams of water, which yields its fruit in season and whose leaf does not wither" (Psalm 1:3, NIV). Pray that whatever he or she does in life will prosper.

Pay attention to what happens in your spirit as you pray blessings and not curses on the other person, even someone whose relationship with you is strained. Give God plenty of room to work in your mind and heart, expanding your capacity to love people even when they're unlovely. Thank Him for loving you—unconditionally—even when you yourself are difficult to love.

Blessed is the one who does not walk in step with the wicked or stand in the way that sinners take or sit in the company of mockers, but whose delight is in the law of the LORD, and who meditates on his law day and night. That person is like a tree planted by streams of water, which yields its fruit in season and whose leaf does not wither—whatever they do prospers. (Psalm 1:1-3, NIV)

Practice

We hope the previous exercise proved to you that prayer is a perfect starting point, whenever you feel offended or wronged. Nothing is more effective than prayer in clearing our minds, cleaning up our hearts, and opening our hands to receive God's gift of perspective. So the next time life serves up an opportunity to feel wounded or let down (and of course it will), rather than pursuing payback, pursue God through prayer.

Next, consider approaching those who are closest to you with the *best* version of yourself—perhaps with renewed energy and a sense of optimism and creativity. Read pages 199-201 in *Simplify: Ten Practices to Unclutter Your Soul*—the section titled "Deepening Your Inner Circle." Then answer the questions that follow.

1. How well are you prioritizing the people you say mean the most to you? Are you investing adequate time in the relationships that matter most?

2. What experience might you share this week with someone whose companionship you highly value? Are you participating in a hobby, or running errands, or volunteering on behalf of a meaningful cause in the immediate future? Would it work to invite that person to come along?

3. How well are you doing at the give-and-take inherent in all sturdy relationships? Initiating interaction is undoubtedly important, but are you also practicing patience by waiting for the other person to reciprocate? If not, why not?

4. How willing are you to "take off the mask" in your interactions with those closest to you? Does vulnerability feel refreshing or terrifying? What fears or insecurities keep you from disclosing more of your real world to the people who love you the most?

5. Would those who know you best say you are one who "shows up" when crises unfold in their lives? Do you put action to your desire to be helpful and caring? And what about the flip side of that coin: Do you let others care for you when you're hurting? In what ways do you need to grow in these areas?

session 3

NOTES

_____

_____

_____

_____

_____

_____

_____

_____

_____

_____

_____

_____

_____

_____

_____

NOTES

_____

_____

_____

_____

_____

_____

_____

_____

_____

_____

_____

_____

_____

_____

_____

_____

_____

_____

NOTES

_____

_____

_____

_____

_____

_____

_____

_____

_____

_____

_____

_____

_____

_____

_____

_____

NOTES

_____

_____

_____

_____

_____

_____

_____

_____

_____

_____

_____

_____

_____

_____

_____

_____

_____

NOTES

_____

_____

_____

_____

_____

_____

_____

_____

_____

_____

_____

_____

_____

_____

_____

fully surrender

Let God's Word Lead

Life, not as drudgery, but outright dancing—
isn't that what we all crave?
To live and breathe and move and speak
with fluidity,
with certainty,
with grace?
"Your revelation is the tune I dance to,"[1] the psalmist
    says,
proof that drudgery doesn't have to be our lot.
We really can experience dancing.
God is the dance partner ready to lead.

---

[1] Psalm 119:77, MSG.

SUGGESTED READING

Prior to meeting with your group to discuss session 4, read pages 205–284 in *Simplify: Ten Practices to Unclutter Your Soul*, which includes the following chapters:

- Chapter 8: From Drifting to Focused: Claiming God's Call on Your Life
- Chapter 9: From Stuck to Moving On: Welcoming New Seasons in Your Life
- Chapter 10: From Meaningless to Satisfied: The Legacy of a Simplified Life

— • • • —

INTRODUCTION

A mom walked into the kitchen one afternoon and found her teenage daughter and her daughter's best friend sitting at the kitchen table, eating chips and salsa and scrutinizing the friend's new tattoo. Eyeing the delicate Japanese symbol that was now colorfully etched on the girl's hip bone, the mom said, "Wow! Do your parents know you got that done?"

"No way," the young woman said. "And please don't tell them!"

The mom gave assurances that she wouldn't spill the beans. Then, out of curiosity, she asked, "By the way, what does the symbol mean?"

"Honesty," the girl replied.

To espouse truth-telling is one thing. But to actually

live it out? Quite another thing indeed. And yet the kind of long-term, fully-orbed simplification we seek comes only by walking in truth. Jesus said it's this truth that has the power to set us free (John 8:32). To know God's truth is to know true freedom. To know true freedom, we must know God's truth.

Ready for the ultimate step toward simplified living? It's the step of surrender—to God's will. To His ways. To His Word. To truth.

CONVERSATION STARTER

What is a favorite verse of Scripture for you, and why?
How has this verse encouraged you along the way?

———————————— • • • ————————————

VIDEO NOTES

Claiming God's Call on Your Life

Memorizing Scripture: from "pain on a stick" to "positive dividends"

The power of a life verse

If every Christ follower had a Scripture-driven conscious-ness . . .

The Legacy of a Simplified Life

Courage to go God's way

Decisions that lead to focus

The harvest that honors God

The generational blessing of allowing Scripture to lead your life

Getting down to basics

Additional pages for notes can be found on pages 84–87.

DISCUSSION POINTS

1. In this session's opening vignette, you saw how Scripture served as an encouragement to Bucky after he made the decision to distance himself from gang life. Describe a time when God's Word played a significant role in your life during a key decision you made.

2. How much weight do you place on the wisdom found in the Bible—not just at key junctures, but in your everyday life? Are you known as a person whose life is directed by God's Word, or as more of a self-sufficient type?

In life, as on the open water, we need a light that directs us back to safe harbor. Scripture is that light.

---

3. Bill Hybels says that having a life verse is critical for maintaining a simplified life. If you already have a life

verse, in what ways have you experienced this to be true? If you don't yet have a life verse, what do you think about Bill's assertion?

4. How would you be different if your life verse more fully governed your life? What changes would those who love you clearly see?

Scripture is powerful. And when you have it at the ready, you make a better series of decisions.

---

5. A life verse, Bill says, helps keep Christ followers "dialed in to the purposes of God." How would you describe the purposes of God? How consistently do you feel "dialed in" to them?

6. What practical obstacles—time? energy? desire? something else?—would you have to overcome in order for God's Word to more consistently guide your life?

7. If you're feeling bold, complete this sentence aloud with the group: *The aspect of my life that is most desperately in need of God's leadership is . . .*

When you have a Scripture-driven consciousness, it motivates you to live in alignment with God's will.

THE CHALLENGE

Find a Life Verse . . . and Use It

[Leader, read this part to the group:] *The challenge this week is to find a life verse (if you don't already have one) and start living it out. To help you begin, describe for the group the kind of person you hope to be a month from now, six months from now, and a year from now, as you allow God's Word to govern your life. What three adjectives do you hope will become true of you?*

- _____

- _____

- _____

[Leader: At this point, you may end the group meeting with a closing prayer. The rest of the exercises in this session are for group members to complete on their own.]

Your Turn

For help in selecting a life verse, see the appendix on pages 285–288 in *Simplify: Ten Practices to Unclutter Your Soul.* Also, scan the Life Verse Catalog (pages 289–301), circling the categories or specific verses that feel most relevant to your current station in life. Then narrow the search to your top three.

On the lines that follow, jot down the three verses. Now that you see them here, is there one that jumps out at you, one you might claim as a life verse for the particular season you're in? Place a check mark next to that one.

LIFE VERSES: MY TOP THREE

1. _____

_____

_____

_____

2. _____

_____

_____

_____

3. _____

_____

_____

Finally, consider the ways in which you can "live out" this verse this week. Factor in the places you typically go and the people you usually see. What would this verse look like "with skin on" for you? Note your ideas in the space below.

To delve more deeply into the concept of a life verse, read pages 205–224 in *Simplify: Ten Practices to Unclutter Your Soul*.

session 4

on your own

This section is intended to help you incorporate the video content and group discussion material into your daily life. The three segments—*Ponder*, *Pray*, and *Practice*—may be completed all at once or spread out over several days.

Ponder

Set aside time after your group meeting to reflect on the questions below. You'll find additional space for journaling on pages 84–87.

> In what category of your life are you most prone to making unwise decisions? Finances? Relationships? Health habits? Something else?

> How open are you to surrendering this particular aspect of life to God's leadership? How willing are you to allow God's Word—His divine wisdom—to lead the way?

Whom can you enlist as a fellow sojourner on the path toward "wising up" in this aspect of your life? Is there a friend or colleague, a trusted family member, a counselor or adviser, or someone else who will cheer you on toward success?

_____

[God said,] "I will honor those who honor me."
(1 Samuel 2:30)

_____

Pray

Based on your responses in the previous section, what is it you really want to see God do in the needy areas of your life? What progress do you hope to make? Jot down your thoughts in the form of a prayer in the space below.

Practice

Psalm 119 highlights a series of fantastic promises made to those who live by the Word of God. Read the psalm in your Bible and answer the following questions.

1. Which phrases seem to leap out at you, and why?

2. This psalm implies it is possible to live a life without regrets when we align ourselves with God's counsel. What regrets do you carry from living life in opposition to God's counsel? How might regrets about the past motivate future changes?

3. What words of wisdom do you think God is trying to speak to you today?

4. Take inventory of the past four weeks (while you've been engaged in this study). How have you begun to implement the principles in *Simplify: Ten Practices to Unclutter Your Soul*?

5. Going forward, which principles and practices are you most likely to leverage in your life? How will you do this?

You're blessed when you stay on course, walking steadily on the road revealed by GOD. You're blessed when you follow his directions, doing your best to find him. (Psalm 119:1-2, MSG)

---

session 4

NOTES

_____

_____

_____

_____

_____

_____

_____

_____

_____

_____

_____

_____

_____

_____

NOTES

_____

_____

_____

_____

_____

_____

_____

_____

_____

_____

_____

_____

_____

_____

_____

_____

NOTES

_____

_____

_____

_____

_____

_____

_____

_____

_____

_____

_____

_____

_____

_____

_____

_____

_____

_____

NOTES

_____

_____

_____

_____

_____

_____

_____

_____

_____

_____

_____

_____

We are merely moving shadows,

and all our busy rushing ends in nothing.

Psalm 39:6

about the authors

Bill Hybels is the founding and senior pastor of Willow Creek Community Church in South Barrington, Illinois, one of the largest and most influential churches in North America. He is the bestselling author of more than twenty books, including *Just Walk Across the Room, Too Busy Not to Pray, Becoming a Contagious Christian, Axiom, Holy Discontent*, and *The Power of a Whisper*.

Hybels is chair of the board for the Willow Creek Association, a not-for-profit organization that equips and empowers more than 15,000 Christian churches from 90 denominations. Each year, he convenes the Global Leadership Summit (GLS), a two-day, world-class leadership event that trains 190,000 leaders in 105 countries. With almost two million participants to date, the GLS is the largest leadership event in the world.

An exceptional communicator, Hybels speaks around the world on strategic issues related to leadership, personal growth, and building thriving churches. He holds a bachelor's degree in biblical studies and an honorary doctorate of divinity from Trinity College in Deerfield, Illinois. He and his wife, Lynne, have two grown children and two grandsons.

Ashley Wiersma is a freelance writer and video producer of Christian living, leadership, and spiritual memoir products. She lives with her husband and daughter in Monument, Colorado.

WILLOW CREEK ASSOCIATION

Vision, Inspiration, and Resources for Church Leaders Worldwide

Founded in 1992, the Willow Creek Association (WCA) serves pastors and leaders through world-class experiences and resources. WCA is committed to a singular idea: that inspired, encouraged, and equipped Christian leaders create thriving local churches that impact their communities for Christ.

In addition to the Global Leadership Summit (WCA's two-day, world-class anchor event), we share ideas and build partnerships. Through the Global Leadership Summit, WCA membership, and strategic partners, we deliver vision and inspiration to more than 190,000 leaders in 650+ cities and 105 countries.

Learn more about WCA's leadership resources and experiences at willowcreek.com.

Willow Creek Association
P.O. Box 3188
Barrington, IL 60011-3188
Phone: 800-570-9812
willowcreek.com